in all Caps!

This exciting collection of crocheted headgear is the creative invention of Drew Emborsky. Included are a stocking cap, tam, bucket hat, beret, striped cap, and headband—each perfect for the woman who loves original style!

Drew Emborsky, aka The Crochet Dude®, was taught to crochet at age five by his mom while snowbound in Lake Tahoe. After studying fine art in college and doing the "starving artist" thing for years, he found solace in crocheting for charity while grieving the passing of his mom. It was during this time with the charity group that he became known as The Crochet Dude, which then led to

the launch of his wildly popular blog, www.thecrochetdude.com. Since then, Drew has published numerous patterns in magazines and compilation books, his own full-length books, appeared as a guest on various TV programs, and is currently the crochet expert on the hit PBS show "Knit and Crochet Today." Drew lives in Houston, Texas with his cats Chandler and Cleocatra.

LEISURE ARTS, INC.
Maumelle, Arkansas

M000084584

Basketweave Stocking Cap

Finished Size: 20¼" (51.5 cm) circumference

■■□□ EASY +

MATERIALS

Medium Weight Yarn

MEDIUM 4

[3 ounces, 185 yards
(85 grams, 170 meters) per skein]: 1 skein
*Photo model made with CARON® COUNTRY #0018
Spice House.*
Crochet hook, size H (5 mm) **or** size needed for gauge
Yarn needle

GAUGE: In Brim pattern,
12 sts = 2¾" (7 cm); 10 rows = 4" (10 cm)
In Crown pattern, 15 sts and 10 rows = 4" (10 cm)

Gauge Swatch: 2¾"w x 4"h (7 cm x 10 cm)
Work same as Brim for 10 rows.

STITCH GUIDE

BACK POST DOUBLE CROCHET *(abbreviated BPdc)*
YO, insert hook from **back** to **front** around post of st
indicated *(Fig. 3, page 31)*, YO and pull up a loop (3 loops
on hook), (YO and draw through 2 loops on hook) twice.
FRONT POST DOUBLE CROCHET *(abbreviated FPdc)*
YO, insert hook from **front** to **back** around post of st
indicated *(Fig. 3, page 31)*, YO and pull up a loop (3 loops
on hook), (YO and draw through 2 loops on hook) twice.
LINKED DOUBLE CROCHET *(abbreviated Ldc)*
Insert hook in side of last st made *(Fig. A, page 3)*, YO and
pull up a loop, insert hook in next st, YO and pull up a loop
(3 loops on hook), (YO and draw through 2 loops on hook)
twice.

Fig. A

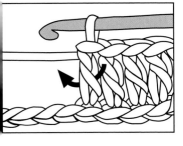

LINKED DOUBLE CROCHET DECREASE *(abbreviated Ldc decrease)*

Insert hook in side of last st made *(Fig. A)*, YO and pull up a loop, (insert hook in next st, YO and pull up a loop) twice (4 loops on hook), YO and draw through 3 loops on hook, YO and draw through remaining 2 loops on hook **(counts as one Ldc).**

Instructions begin on page 4.

BRIM
Ch 14.

Row 1 (Right side)**:** Dc in fourth ch from hook **(3 skipped chs count as first dc)** and in each ch across: 12 dc.

Note: Loop a short piece of yarn around any stitch to mark Row 1 as **right** side.

Row 2: Ch 2 **(counts as first hdc, now and throughout),** turn; work BPdc around each of next 2 dc, (work FPdc around each of next 2 dc, work BPdc around each of next 2 dc) twice, hdc in last dc.

Rows 3 and 4: Ch 2, turn; work FPdc around each of next 2 sts, (work BPdc around each of next 2 sts, work FPdc around each of next 2 sts) twice, hdc in last hdc.

Rows 5 and 6: Ch 2, turn; work BPdc around each of next 2 sts, (work FPdc around each of next 2 sts, work BPdc around each of next 2 sts) twice, hdc in last hdc.

Rows 7-53: Repeat Rows 3-6, 11 times; then repeat Rows 3-5 once **more.**

Finish off, leaving a long end for sewing.

Thread yarn needle with long end. With **right** sides together and matching top of sts on Row 53 with free loops of beginning ch *(Fig. 1, page 31)*, sew seam.

CROWN

Rnd 1: With **wrong** side of Brim facing and working in end of rows, join yarn with sc in first row *(see Joining With Sc, page 30)*; work 75 sc evenly spaced around; do **not** join, place a marker to mark the beginning of the round *(see Markers, page 30)*: 76 sc.

Rnd 2 (Turning ridge)**:** Sc in Front Loop Only of next sc *(Fig. 2, page 31)* and each sc around.

Rnds 3-12: Work Ldc in next st and in each st around.

SHAPING

Rnd 1: (Work Ldc in next 2 sts, work Ldc decrease) around: 57 Ldc.

Rnd 2: (Work Ldc in next 2 sts, work Ldc decrease) 14 times, work Ldc in next st: 43 Ldc.

Rnd 3: Work Ldc in next st, work Ldc decrease, (work Ldc in next 2 sts, work Ldc decrease) around: 32 Ldc.

Rnd 4: (Work Ldc in next 2 sts, work Ldc decrease) around: 24 Ldc.

Rnd 5: (Work Ldc in next 2 sts, work Ldc decrease) around: 18 Ldc.

Rnd 6: Work Ldc decrease, (work Ldc in next 2 sts, work Ldc decrease) around; slip st in next Ldc, finish off leaving a long end for sewing: 13 Ldc.

Thread yarn needle with long end and weave through sts on Rnd 6; gather **tightly** and secure end.

Turn Brim up along turning ridge.

Cabled Tam

Finished Size: 21" (53.5 cm) circumference

◼◼◻◻ EASY

MATERIALS

Medium Weight Yarn

MEDIUM 4

[3 ounces, 185 yards
(85 grams, 170 meters) per skein]: 1 skein
Photo model made with CARON® COUNTRY #0016 Charcoal.
Crochet hook, size I (5.5 mm) **or** size needed for gauge

GAUGE: In Ribbing pattern,
20 sts and 10 rows = 4" (10 cm)

Gauge Swatch: 3½" (9 cm) diameter
Work same as Crown for 4 rnds.

STITCH GUIDE

BACK POST DOUBLE CROCHET *(abbreviated BPdc)*
YO, insert hook from **back** to **front** around post of st
indicated *(Fig. 3, page 31)*, YO and pull up a loop (3 loops
on hook), (YO and draw through 2 loops on hook) twice.
FRONT POST DOUBLE CROCHET *(abbreviated FPdc)*
YO, insert hook from **front** to **back** around post of st
indicated *(Fig. 3, page 31)*, YO and pull up a loop (3 loops
on hook), (YO and draw through 2 loops on hook) twice.
CABLE (uses next 2 sts)
Skip next st, work FPdc around next st, working in **front** of
FPdc just made, work FPdc around skipped st.

CROWN

Ch 4; join with slip st to form a ring.

Rnd 1 (Right side): Ch 3 **(counts as first dc)**, 15 dc in ring;
join with slip st to first dc: 16 dc.

Rnd 2: Ch 2 (counts as first hdc, now and throughout), work 2 FPdc around next dc, (work BPdc around next dc, work 2 FPdc around next dc) around; join with slip st to first hdc: 24 sts.

Rnd 3: Ch 2, work FPdc around next st, work 2 FPdc around next st, ★ work BPdc around next st, work FPdc around next st, work 2 FPdc around next st; repeat from ★ around; join with slip st to first hdc: 32 sts.

Instructions continued on page 8.

Rnd 4: Ch 2, work FPdc around each of next 2 sts, work 2 FPdc around next st, ★ work BPdc around next st, work FPdc around each of next 2 sts, work 2 FPdc around next st; repeat from ★ around; join with slip st to first hdc: 40 sts.

Rnd 5: Ch 2, work FPdc around next st, work Cable, work 2 FPdc around next st, ★ work BPdc around next st, work FPdc around next st, work Cable, work 2 FPdc around next st; repeat from ★ around; join with slip st to first hdc: 48 sts.

Rnd 6: Ch 2, work FPdc around next st, work Cable, work BPdc around next st, work 2 FPdc around next st, ★ work BPdc around next st, work FPdc around next st, work Cable, work BPdc around next st, work 2 FPdc around next st; repeat from ★ around; join with slip st to first hdc: 56 sts.

Rnd 7: Ch 2, work FPdc around next st, work Cable, work BPdc around next st, work FPdc around next st, work 2 FPdc around next st, ★ work BPdc around next st, work FPdc around next st, work Cable, work BPdc around next st, work FPdc around next st, work 2 FPdc around next st; repeat from ★ around; join with slip st to first hdc: 64 sts.

Rnd 8: Ch 2, work FPdc around next st, work Cable, work BPdc around next st, work Cable, work 2 FPdc around next st, ★ work BPdc around next st, work FPdc around next st, work Cable, work BPdc around next st, work Cable, work 2 FPdc around next st; repeat from ★ around; join with slip st to first hdc: 72 sts.

Rnd 9: Ch 2, work FPdc around next st, (work Cable, work BPdc around next st) twice, work 2 FPdc around next st, ★ work BPdc around next st, work FPdc around next st, (work Cable, work BPdc around next st) twice, work 2 FPdc around next st; repeat from ★ around; join with slip st to first hdc: 80 sts.

Rnd 10: Ch 2, work FPdc around next st, (work Cable, work BPdc around next st) twice, work FPdc around next st, work 2 FPdc around next st, ★ work BPdc around next st, work FPdc around next st, (work Cable, work BPdc around next st) twice, work FPdc around next st, work 2 FPdc around next st; repeat from ★ around; join with slip st to first hdc: 88 sts.

Rnd 11: Ch 2, work FPdc around next st, work Cable, (work BPdc around next st, work Cable) twice, work 2 FPdc around next st, ★ work BPdc around next st, work FPdc around next st, work Cable, (work BPdc around next st, work Cable) twice, work 2 FPdc around next st; repeat from ★ around; join with slip st to first hdc: 96 sts.

Rnd 12: Ch 2, work FPdc around next st, (work Cable, work BPdc around next st) 3 times, work 2 FPdc around next st, ★ work BPdc around next st, work FPdc around next st, (work Cable, work BPdc around next st) 3 times, work 2 FPdc around next st; repeat from ★ around; join with slip st to first hdc: 104 sts.

Rnd 13: Ch 2, work FPdc around each of next 3 sts, (work BPdc around next st, work FPdc around each of next 2 sts) 3 times, ★ work BPdc around next st, work FPdc around each of next 3 sts, (work BPdc around next st, work FPdc around each of next 2 sts) 3 times; repeat from ★ around; join with slip st to first hdc.

RIBBING

Rnd 1: Working in Back Loops Only *(Fig. 2, page 31)*, slip st in next st, ch 3 **(counts as first dc)**, (dc in next 2 sts, skip next st) 4 times, ★ dc in next 3 sts, skip next st, (dc in next 2 sts, skip next st) 3 times; repeat from ★ around; join with slip st to first dc: 72 dc.

Rnds 2-7: Ch 2, work FPdc around next st, (work BPdc around next st, work FPdc around next st) around; join with slip st to first hdc.

Finish off.

Reversible Cabled Headband

Finished Size:
4" wide x 20" circumference
(10 cm x 51 cm)

◖■□□ **EASY**

MATERIALS

MEDIUM **4**

Medium Weight Yarn
[3 ounces, 185 yards
(85 grams, 170 meters) per skein]: 1 skein
*Photo model made with CARON® COUNTRY #0022
    Plum Pudding.*
Crochet hook, size H (5 mm) **or** size needed for gauge
Yarn needle

GAUGE SWATCH: 4" (10 cm) square
Work same as Headband through Row 11.

STITCH GUIDE

BACK POST DOUBLE CROCHET *(abbreviated BPdc)*
YO, insert hook from **back** to **front** around post of st
indicated *(Fig. 3, page 31)*, YO and pull up a loop (3 loops
on hook), (YO and draw through 2 loops on hook) twice.
FRONT POST DOUBLE CROCHET *(abbreviated FPdc)*
YO, insert hook from **front** to **back** around post of st
indicated *(Fig. 3, page 31)*, YO and pull up a loop (3 loops
on hook), (YO and draw through 2 loops on hook) twice.
CABLE (uses next 2 sts)
Skip next st, work FPdc around next st, working in **front** of
FPdc just made, work FPdc around skipped st.

Instructions begin on page 12.

HEADBAND
Ch 26.

Row 1: Dc in fourth ch from hook **(3 skipped chs count as first dc)** and in each ch across: 24 dc.

Row 2: Ch 2 **(counts as first hdc, now and throughout)**, turn; work BPdc around each of next 2 dc, (work FPdc around each of next 2 dc, work BPdc around each of next 2 dc) across to last dc, hdc in last dc.

Row 3: Ch 2, turn; work Cable, (work BPdc around each of next 2 sts, work Cable) across to last hdc, hdc in last hdc.

Row 4: Ch 2, turn; work BPdc around each of next 2 sts, (work Cable, work BPdc around each of next 2 sts) across to last hdc, hdc in last hdc.

Repeat Rows 3 and 4 for pattern until piece measures approximately 20" (51 cm) from beginning ch, ending by working Row 3.

Finish off, leaving a long end for sewing.

Thread yarn needle with long end; matching sts of last row with free loops of beginning ch *(Fig. 1, page 31)*, sew seam; weave yarn in and out of seam, gather seam up **tightly** to measure 2" (5 cm) and secure end.

Shearling Bucket Hat

Shown on page 15.
Finished Size: 20¼" (51.5 cm) circumference

◖■■◻◲ EASY +

MATERIALS

Medium Weight Yarn
[3 ounces, 185 yards
(85 grams, 170 meters) per skein]:
Brown and Natural - 1 skein **each** color
*Photo model made with CARON® COUNTRY #0019
    Vicuna & #0007 Naturally.*
Crochet hook, size I (5.5 mm) **or** size needed for gauge
Yarn needle

GAUGE: In Crown pattern, 15 sts and 12 rnds = 4" (10 cm)

Gauge Swatch: 4¼"w x 4"h (10.75 cm x 10 cm)
With Brown, ch 18.
Row 1: Dc in fourth ch from hook **(3 skipped chs count as first dc)** and in each ch across: 16 dc.
Rows 2-12: Ch 2 **(counts as first hdc)**, turn; (work FPdc around next st, work BPdc around next st) across to last st, hdc in last st.
Finish off.

Continued on page 14.

STITCH GUIDE
LOOP STITCH

Insert the hook in the next stitch, wrap the yarn around the index finger of the left hand 2 times **more**, insert hook through all loops on finger following the direction indicated by arrow *(Fig. A)*, being careful to hook all loops *(Fig. B)*, draw through stitch, remove finger from loops, YO and draw through all 4 loops on hook pulling each loop to measure approximately 2" (5 cm) **(Loop St made,** *Fig. C).*

Fig. A

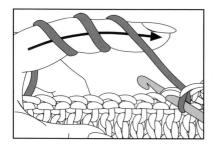

Fig. B

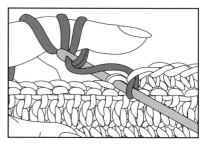

Fig. C

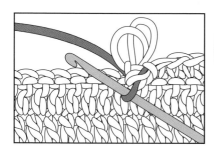

Instructions begin on page 16.

BACK POST DOUBLE CROCHET *(abbreviated BPdc)*
YO, insert hook from **back** to **front** around post of st indicated *(Fig. 3, page 1)*, YO and pull up a loop (3 loops on hook), (YO and draw through 2 loops on hook) twice.
FRONT POST DOUBLE CROCHET *(abbreviated FPdc)*
YO, insert hook from **front** to **back** around post of st indicated *(Fig. 3, page 1)*, YO and pull up a loop (3 loops on hook), (YO and draw through 2 loops on hook) twice.
DECREASE (uses next 3 sts)
YO, insert hook from **front** to **back** around post of next st, YO and pull up a loop, YO and draw through 2 loops on hook, YO, skip next st, insert hook from **front** to **back** around post of next st, YO and pull up a loop, YO and draw through 2 loops on hook, YO and draw through all 3 loops on hook **(counts as one FPdc).**

BRIM
Note: Make 2 equal size balls from skein of Natural **or** pull one strand from the inside and one strand from the outside of the skein to create a double strand.

With a double strand of Natural, ch 76; being sure **not** to twist ch, join with slip st to form a ring.

Rnd 1: Ch 1, work Loop St in each ch around; do **not** join, place a marker to mark the beginning of the rnd *(see Markers, page 30)*: 76 sts.

Rnd 2: Work Loop St in each st around.

Rnd 3 (Right side)**:** Fold piece to match sts on Rnd 2 with free loops of beginning ch *(Fig. 1, page 31)*, keeping loops to outside; working through **both** thicknesses, sc in each st around; join with slip st to first sc, finish off: 76 sc.

Note: Loop a short piece of yarn around any stitch to mark Rnd 3 as **right** side.

CROWN

Rnd 1: With **right** side facing and working in Back Loops Only *(Fig. 2, page 31)*, join single strand of Brown with sc in any sc on Rnd 3 of Brim *(see Joining With Sc, page 30)*; sc in each sc around; join with slip st to **both** loops of first sc.

Rnd 2: Ch 3 **(counts as first dc)**, dc in both loops of next sc and each sc around; join with slip st to first dc.

Rnds 3-17: Ch 2 **(counts as first hdc, now and throughout)**, work FPdc around next st, (work BPdc around next st, work FPdc around next st) around; join with slip st to first hdc.

Rnd 18: Ch 2, decrease, (work BPdc around next st, decrease) around; join with slip st to first hdc: 38 sts.

Rnd 19: Ch 2, (decrease, work BPdc around next st) 9 times, work FPdc around next st; join with slip st to first hdc, finish off leaving a long end for sewing: 20 sts.

Thread yarn needle with long end and weave through sts on Rnd 19; gather **tightly** and secure end.

Cut all loops on Brim and brush lightly to separate plies.

Slouchy Beret

Finished Size: 21" (53.5 cm) circumference

■■□□ **EASY**

MATERIALS
Medium Weight Yarn **4**
[3 ounces, 185 yards
(85 grams, 170 meters) per skein]: 2 skeins
Photo model made with CARON® COUNTRY #0010 Sunset.
Crochet hook, size H (5 mm) **or** size needed for gauge
Yarn needle

GAUGE: In Crown pattern (Rnds 6-11),
18 sts = 4" (10 cm); 12 rows = 3" (7.5 cm)
In Ribbing, 5 sts = 1" (2.5 cm); 10 rows = 3" (7.5 cm)

Gauge Swatch: 1"w x 3"h (2.5 cm x 7.5 cm)
Ch 6.
Work same as Ribbing for 10 rows.

STITCH GUIDE
BOBBLE (uses one st)
Insert hook in st indicated, YO and pull up a loop (2 loops
on hook), (YO and draw through one loop on hook) 3 times
(ch 3 made), YO and draw through both loops on hook.
BEGINNING CABLE (uses 3 sts)
Ch 3 **(counts as first dc)**, dc in next st, working in **front** of
2 dc just made, dc in st before first dc.
CABLE (uses next 3 sts)
Skip next st, dc in next 2 sts, working in **front** of dc just
made, dc in skipped st.
DECREASE (uses next 2 sc)
Pull up a loop in next 2 sts, YO and draw through all
3 loops on hook **(counts as one sc)**.

RIBBING
Ch 6.

Row 1: Sc in second ch from hook and in each ch across: 5 sc.

Rows 2-70: Ch 1, turn; sc in Back Loop Only of each sc across *(Fig. 2, page 31)*; do **not** finish off.

CROWN
Rnd 1 (Right side)**:** Ch 1, do **not** turn; sc in end of each row across; join with slip st to first sc: 70 sc.

Instructions continued on page 20.

Rnd 2: Ch 1, sc in same st as joining, work Bobble in next sc, (sc in next sc, work Bobble in next sc) around; join with slip st to first sc: 35 sc and 35 Bobbles.

Rnd 3: Ch 1, sc in same st as joining and in each st around; join with slip st to first sc: 70 sc.

Rnd 4: Ch 1, 2 sc in same st as joining, work Bobble in next sc, (2 sc in next sc, work Bobble in next sc) around; join with slip st to first sc: 70 sc and 35 Bobbles.

Rnd 5: Ch 1, sc in same st as joining and in each st around; join with slip st to first sc: 105 sc.

Rnd 6: Work Beginning Cable, work Cables around; join with slip st to first dc: 35 Cables.

Rnd 7: Ch 1, sc in same st as joining and in each st around; join with slip st to first sc: 105 sc.

Rnd 8: Ch 1, sc in same st as joining and in next sc, work Bobble in next sc, (sc in next 2 sc, work Bobble in next sc) around; join with slip st to first sc: 70 sc and 35 Bobbles.

Rnds 9-11: Repeat Rnds 7 and 8 once, then repeat Rnd 7 once **more**: 105 sc.

Rnds 12-25: Repeat Rnds 6-11 twice, then repeat Rnds 6 and 7 once **more**: 105 sc.

SHAPING
Rnd 1: Ch 1, decrease beginning in same st as joining, work Bobble in next sc, (decrease, work Bobble in next sc) around; join with slip st to first sc: 35 sc and 35 Bobbles.

Rnd 2: Ch 1, sc in same st as joining and in each st around; join with slip st to first sc: 70 sc.

Rnd 3: Ch 1, sc in same st as joining, work Bobble in next sc, (sc in next sc, work Bobble in next sc) around; join with slip st to first sc: 35 sc and 35 Bobbles.

Rnd 4: Ch 1, decrease beginning in same st as joining, sc in next st and in each st around; join with slip st to first sc: 69 sc.

Rnd 5: Work Beginning Cable, work Cables around; join with slip st to first dc: 23 Cables.

Rnd 6: Ch 1, sc in same st as joining and in each st around; join with slip st to first sc: 69 sc.

Rnd 7: Ch 1, decrease beginning in same st as joining, work Bobble in next sc, (decrease, work Bobble in next sc) around; join with slip st to first sc: 23 sc and 23 Bobbles.

Rnd 8: Ch 1, sc in same st as joining and in each st around; join with slip st to first sc: 46 sc.

Rnd 9: Ch 1, sc in same st as joining, work Bobble in next sc, (sc in next sc, work Bobble in next sc) around; join with slip st to first sc: 23 sc and 23 Bobbles.

Rnd 10: Ch 1, decrease beginning in same st as joining, decrease around; join with slip st to first sc, finish off leaving a long end for sewing: 23 sc.

Thread yarn needle with long end and weave through sts on Rnd 10; gather **tightly** and secure end.

With **wrong** sides together, sew Ribbing seam working in outside loops of Row 70 and in free loops of beginning ch *(Fig. 1, page 31)*.

Stripes and Cables Hat

Finished Size: 20¼" (51.5 cm) circumference

◼◼◻◻ EASY

MATERIALS
Medium Weight Yarn
[3 ounces, 185 yards
(85 grams, 170 meters) per skein]:
Turquoise and Natural - 1 skein **each** color
*Photo model made with CARON® COUNTRY #0021 Peacock
    & #0007 Naturally.*
Crochet hook, size I (5.5 mm) **or** size needed for gauge
Safety pins - 2
Yarn needle

GAUGE: In pattern, 16 sts and 12 rows = 4" (10 cm)

Gauge Swatch: 4" (10 cm) square
With Turquoise, ch 18.
Row 1: Dc in fourth ch from hook **(3 skipped chs count as first dc)** and in each ch across: 16 dc.
Rows 2-12: Ch 2 **(counts as first hdc)**, (work FPdc around next st, work BPdc around next st) across to last st, hdc in last st.
Finish off.

STITCH GUIDE
BACK POST DOUBLE CROCHET *(abbreviated BPdc)*
YO, insert hook from **back** to **front** around post of st indicated *(Fig. 3, page 31)*, YO and pull up a loop (3 loops on hook), (YO and draw through 2 loops on hook) twice.
FRONT POST DOUBLE CROCHET *(abbreviated FPdc)*
YO, insert hook from **front** to **back** around post of st indicated *(Fig. 3, page 31)*, YO and pull up a loop (3 loops on hook), (YO and draw through 2 loops on hook) twice.

CABLE (uses next 3 sts)
Skip next 2 sts, work FPdc around next st, working in **front** of FPdc just made, work FPdc around second skipped st, working in **front** of last FPdc made, work FPdc around first skipped st.

Instructions begin on page 24.

HAT

With Turquoise, ch 81; being careful **not** to twist ch, join with slip st to form a ring.

Rnd 1 (Right side)**:** Ch 3 **(counts as first dc)**, dc in next ch and in each ch around; join with slip st to first dc: 81 dc.

Note: Loop a short piece of yarn around any stitch to mark Rnd 1 as **right** side.

Rnds 2 and 3: Ch 2 **(counts as first hdc, now and throughout)**, work BPdc around next st, work FPdc around each of next 2 sts, work BPdc around each of next 2 sts, work FPdc around each of next 3 sts, ★ work BPdc around each of next 2 sts, work FPdc around each of next 2 sts, work BPdc around each of next 2 sts, work FPdc around each of next 3 sts; repeat from ★ around; join with slip st to first hdc.

Rnd 4: Ch 2, work BPdc around next st, work FPdc around each of next 2 sts, work BPdc around each of next 2 sts, work Cable, ★ work BPdc around each of next 2 sts, work FPdc around each of next 2 sts, work BPdc around each of next 2 sts, work Cable; repeat from ★ around; join with slip st to first hdc.

Rnd 5: Ch 2, work BPdc around next st, work FPdc around each of next 2 sts, work BPdc around each of next 2 sts, work FPdc around each of next 3 sts, ★ work BPdc around each of next 2 sts, work FPdc around each of next 2 sts, work BPdc around each of next 2 sts, work FPdc around each of next 3 sts; repeat from ★ around; join with slip st to first hdc, place loop from hook onto safety pin to keep piece from unraveling while working the next rnd, hold Turquoise to **wrong** side of work.

Rnd 6: With **right** side facing, join Natural with dc from **back** to **front** around post of first hdc (same st as joining) *(see Joining With Dc, page 30)*; work BPdc around next st, work FPdc around each of next 2 sts, work BPdc around each of next 2 sts, work Cable, ★ work BPdc around each of next 2 sts, work FPdc around each of next 2 sts, work BPdc around each of next 2 sts, work Cable; repeat from ★ around; join with slip st to first dc.

Rnd 7: Ch 2, work BPdc around next st, work FPdc around each of next 2 sts, work BPdc around each of next 2 sts, work FPdc around each of next 3 sts, ★ work BPdc around each of next 2 sts, work FPdc around each of next 2 sts, work BPdc around each of next 2 sts, work FPdc around each of next 3 sts; repeat from ★ around; join with slip st to first hdc, place loop from hook onto safety pin to keep piece from unraveling while working the next rnd, hold Natural to **wrong** side of work.

Rnd 8: With **right** side facing, slip Turquoise loop from safety pin onto hook, ch 3 (at back of work); work BPdc around each of first 2 sts (same st as joining and next BPdc), work FPdc around each of next 2 sts, work BPdc around each of next 2 sts, work Cable, ★ work BPdc around each of next 2 sts, work FPdc around each of next 2 sts, work BPdc around each of next 2 sts, work Cable; repeat from ★ around; skip beginning ch-3 and join with slip st to next BPdc.

Rnd 9: Ch 2, work BPdc around next st, work FPdc around each of next 2 sts, work BPdc around each of next 2 sts, work FPdc around each of next 3 sts, ★ work BPdc around each of next 2 sts, work FPdc around each of next 2 sts, work BPdc around each of next 2 sts, work FPdc around each of next 3 sts; repeat from ★ around; join with slip st to first hdc, place loop from hook onto safety pin to keep piece from unraveling while working the next rnd, hold Turquoise to **wrong** side of work.

Instructions continued on page 26.

Rnd 10: With **right** side facing, slip Natural loop from safety pin onto hook, ch 3 (at back of work); work BPdc around each of first 2 sts (same st as joining and next BPdc), work FPdc around each of next 2 sts, work BPdc around each of next 2 sts, work Cable, ★ work BPdc around each of next 2 sts, work FPdc around each of next 2 sts, work BPdc around each of next 2 sts, work Cable; repeat from ★ around; skip beginning ch-3 and join with slip st to next BPdc.

Rnds 11-18: Repeat Rnds 7-10 twice.

Rnd 19: Ch 2, work BPdc around **both** of first 2 sts (decrease made), work FPdc around each of next 2 sts, work BPdc around **both** of next 2 sts (decrease made), work FPdc around each of next 3 sts, ★ work BPdc around **both** of next 2 sts (decrease made), work FPdc around each of next 2 sts, work BPdc around **both** of next 2 sts (decrease made), work FPdc around each of next 3 sts; repeat from ★ around; skip first hdc and join with slip st to next BPdc, place loop from hook onto safety pin to keep piece from unraveling while working the next rnd, hold Natural to **wrong** side of work: 63 sts.

Rnd 20: With **right** side facing, slip Turquoise loop from safety pin onto hook, ch 3 (at back of work); work BPdc around first BPdc, work FPdc around each of next 2 sts, work BPdc around next st, work Cable, ★ work BPdc around next st, work FPdc around each of next 2 sts, work BPdc around next st, work Cable; repeat from ★ around; skip beginning ch-3 and join with slip st to next BPdc.

Rnd 21: Ch 2, work BPdc around **both** of first 2 sts (ch-3 and BPdc), work FPdc around **both** of next 2 sts (decrease made), work BPdc around next st, work FPdc around each of next 3 sts, ★ work BPdc around next st, work FPdc around **both** of next 2 sts (decrease made),

work BPdc around next st, work FPdc around each of next 3 sts; repeat from ★ around; skip first hdc and join with slip st to next BPdc, finish off Turquoise: 54 sts.

Rnd 22: With **right** side facing, slip Natural loop from safety pin onto hook, ch 3 (at back of work); work BPdc around first 2 sts (hdc and BPdc), work FPdc around next st, work BPdc around next st, work Cable, ★ work BPdc around next st, work FPdc around next st, work BPdc around next st, work Cable; repeat from ★ around; skip beginning ch-3 and join with slip st to next BPdc.

Rnd 23: Ch 2, work BPdc around first 2 sts (ch-3 and BPdc), work FPdc around next st, work BPdc around next st, work FPdc around each of next 3 sts, ★ work BPdc around next st, work FPdc around next st, work BPdc around next st, work FPdc around each of next 3 sts; repeat from ★ around; skip first hdc and join with slip st to next BPdc, finish off leaving a long ending for sewing.

Thread yarn needle with long end and weave through sts on Rnd 23; gather **tightly** and secure end.

Make a 3¹/₂" (9 cm) pom-pom using both colors *(Figs. 4a-c, page 32)*. Sew to top of Hat.

GENERAL INSTRUCTIONS

ABBREVIATIONS

BPdc   Back Post double crochet(s)
ch(s)   chain(s)
cm   centimeters
dc   double crochet(s)
FPdc   Front Post double crochet(s)
hdc   half double crochet(s)
Ldc   Linked double crochet(s)
mm   millimeters
Rnd(s) Round(s)
sc   single crochet(s)
st(s)   stitch(es)
YO   yarn over

★ — work instructions following ★ as many **more** times as indicated in addition to the first time.

( ) or [ ] — work enclosed instructions **as many** times as specified by the number immediately following **or** work all enclosed instructions in the stitch or space indicated **or** contains explanatory remarks.

colon (:) — the number(s) given after a colon at the end of a row or round denote(s) the number of stitches or spaces you should have on that row or round.

CROCHET HOOKS												
U.S.	B-1	C-2	D-3	E-4	F-5	G-6	H-8	I-9	J-10	K-10½	N	P	Q
Metric - mm	2.25	2.75	3.25	3.5	3.75	4	5	5.5	6	6.5	9	10	15

CROCHET TERMINOLOGY	
UNITED STATES	**INTERNATIONAL**
slip stitch (slip st) =	single crochet (sc)
single crochet (sc) =	double crochet (dc)
half double crochet (hdc) =	half treble crochet (htr)
double crochet (dc) =	treble crochet(tr)
treble crochet (tr) =	double treble crochet (dtr)
double treble crochet (dtr) =	triple treble crochet (ttr)
triple treble crochet (tr tr) =	quadruple treble crochet (qtr)
skip =	miss

◼☐☐☐ BEGINNER	Projects for first-time crocheters using basic stitches. Minimal shaping.
◼◼☐☐ EASY	Projects using yarn with basic stitches, repetitive stitch patterns, simple color changes, and simple shaping and finishing.
◼◼◼☐ INTERMEDIATE	Projects using a variety of techniques, such as basic lace patterns or color patterns, mid-level shaping and finishing.
◼◼◼◼ EXPERIENCED	Projects with intricate stitch patterns, techniques and dimension, such as non-repeating patterns, multi-color techniques, fine threads, small hooks, detailed shaping and refined finishing.

Yarn Weight Symbol & Names	LACE 0	SUPER FINE 1	FINE 2	LIGHT 3	MEDIUM 4	BULKY 5	SUPER BULKY 6
Type of Yarns in Category	Fingering, 10-count crochet thread	Sock, Fingering Baby	Sport, Baby	DK, Light Worsted	Worsted, Afghan, Aran	Chunky, Craft, Rug	Bulky, Roving
Crochet Gauge* Ranges in Single Crochet to 4" (10 cm)	32-42 double crochets**	21-32 sts	16-20 sts	12-17 sts	11-14 sts	8-11 sts	5-9 sts
Advised Hook Size Range	Steel*** 6,7,8 Regular hook B-1	B-1 to E-4	E-4 to 7	7 to I-9	I-9 to K-10.5	K-10.5 to M-13	M-13 and larger

*GUIDELINES ONLY: The chart above reflects the most commonly used gauges and hook sizes for specific yarn categories.

** Lace weight yarns are usually crocheted on larger-size hooks to create lacy openwork patterns. Accordingly, a gauge range is difficult to determine. Always follow the gauge stated in your pattern.

*** Steel crochet hooks are sized differently from regular hooks–the higher the number the smaller the hook, which is the reverse of regular hook sizing.

GAUGE

Exact gauge is essential for proper size. Before beginning your piece, make the sample swatch given in the individual instructions in the yarn and hook specified. After completing the swatch, measure it, counting your stitches and rows or rounds carefully. If your swatch is larger or smaller than specified, **make another, changing hook size to get the correct gauge.** Keep trying until you find the size hook that will give you the specified gauge.

MARKERS

Markers are used to help distinguish the beginning of each round being worked. Place a 2" (5 cm) scrap piece of yarn before the first stitch of each round, moving the marker after each round is complete.

JOINING WITH SC

When instructed to join with a sc, begin with a slip knot on the hook. Insert the hook in the stitch or the space indicated, YO and pull up a loop, YO and draw through both loops on hook.

JOINING WITH DC

When instructed to join with a dc, begin with a slip knot on the hook. YO, holding the loop on the hook, insert the hook in the stitch or the space indicated, YO and pull up a loop (3 loops on hook), (YO and draw through 2 loops on hook) twice.

FREE LOOPS OF A CHAIN

When instructed to work in the free loops of a chain, work in the loop indicated by arrow *(Fig. 1)*.

Fig. 1

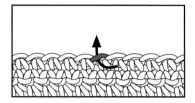

BACK OR FRONT LOOP ONLY

Work only in loop(s) indicated by arrow *(Fig. 2)*.

Fig. 2

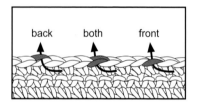

POST STITCH

Work around post of stitch indicated, inserting hook in direction of arrow *(Fig. 3)*.

Fig. 3

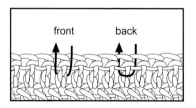

POM-POM

Cut a piece of cardboard 3" (7.5 cm) wide and as long as you want the diameter of your finished pom-pom to be. Wind the yarn around the cardboard until it is approximately ¹/₂" (12 mm) thick in the middle *(Fig. 4a)*. Carefully slip the yarn off the cardboard and firmly tie an 18" (45.5 cm) length of yarn around the middle *(Fig. 4b)*. Leave yarn ends long enough to attach the pom-pom. Cut the loops on both ends and trim the pom-pom into a smooth ball *(Fig. 4c)*.

Fig. 4a   **Fig. 4b**   **Fig. 4c**

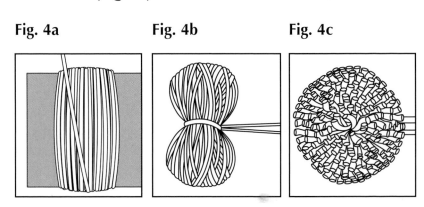

We have made every effort to ensure that these instructions are accurate and complete. We cannot, however, be responsible for human error, typographical mistakes, or variations in individual work.

©2009 by Leisure Arts, Inc., 104 Champs Blvd., Ste. 100, Maumelle, AR 72113. All rights reserved. This publication is protected under federal copyright laws. Reproduction or distribution of this publication or any other Leisure Arts publication, including publications which are out of print, is prohibited unless specifically authorized. This includes, but is not limited to, any form of reproduction or distribution on or through the Internet, including posting, scanning, or e-mail transmission.